Beauty of
Pennsylvania

Beauty of
Pennsylvania

Text: Paul M. Lewis
Concept & Design: Robert D. Shangle

First Printing October, 1990
Published by LTA Publishing Company
2735 S.E. Raymond Street, Portland, Oregon 97202
Robert D. Shangle, Publisher

"Learn about America in a beautiful way."

This book features the photography of
James Blank
and Shangle Photographics

Library of Congress Cataloging-in-Publication Data
Lewis, Paul M.
   Beauty of Pennsylvania / text, Paul M. Lewis.
     p.   cm.
   ISBN 0-917630-87-4: $19.95 — ISBN 0-917630-86-6: $9.95 (pbk.)
   1. Pennsylvnia — Description and travel — 1981 — Views.
  2. Pennsylvania — Description and travel — 1981 — Guide-books.
I. Title.
F150.L48   1989
917.4804'43 — dc20   CIP

Contents

Foundation
Of A Nation

Long before the land in this country became the priceless commodity it is today, people were fighting over it. The soft, green valleys of Pennsylvania were prized for their beauty and fertility by several contesting groups of settlers before, during, and after the Revolution. The Indians were mixed up in the land fuss, too, but in their battles with encroaching settlers, they were just doing what Indians all over the country were to do as the westward migration forced them off their territories. From 1682 settlers were moving into Pennsylvania, under the charter granted William Penn by King Charles II. Their occupancy, in the Susquehanna Valley at least, was challenged by groups of Connecticut Yankees seeking to annex the area to Connecticut. The French and Indian War was fought over portions of this territory; later, some of the primary battles of the American Revolution took place here; and Gettysburg has earned its place as one of the bloodiest of Civil War battlefields.

The Susquehanna Valley has seen its share of these land wars. The Susquehanna River, draining half of the area of the state, is a fabled stream important to both Indian and western cultures. Indian tribes of the Iroquois nation, such as the Susquehannocks, had long dwelt on its banks, raising crops in its fertile loam and feasting on the game of its enfolding forests. The valley has been one of the country's most exquisite examples of lush river environment.

Such a gorgeous extent of river land stretching through the center of a now-densely populated state, should have largely disappeared beneath the factories and mills that line its shores after two centuries of settlement. But this has not happened. There are, of course, cities and indus-

7

tries situated along its shallow, rushing waters. However, for many of its sinuous miles, it consorts only with mountains and meadows whose most numerous inhabitants are the richly diversified wildlife of the idyllic Susquehanna Valley.

The beauty of Pennsylvania's great river is just one aspect of the Keystone State's galaxy of enchantments. The state's good looks are partly a function of the Blue and Allegheny mountains that sweep diagonally across it, in ridge after ridge, from the southwest to the northeast, interrupted in any major way only by the lower Susquehanna River and its North and West branches. The low Alleghenies, rounded off by erosion and glacial pressures over uncounted eons, are a part of the long Appalachian chain that rule almost the whole eastern seaboard back of the coast and the Piedmont.

On the other hand, a lot of Pennsylvania's magic is man-made. Not for nothing is it called the Keystone State. It was in the right place at the right time to play a crucial role in the nation's beginnings. And after we got started, the resources of the state and the vitality of its business enterprises were what kept us going. All around the state there are places that keep reminding us of that. Hallowed parts of its old towns and cities have been carefully preserved or restored, glowing with their own kind of beauty as they become overlaid with the patina of age. Philadelphia, before all else, is history personified. It has managed to keep its traditions — and the nation's — alive through a loving attention to the artifacts and symbols of the early struggles for independence that took place here. But the Quaker City is merely the most noteworthy example of the history that is behind almost every tree in Pennsylvania. Some of our most soul-wrenching dramas as a nation have been enacted upon its rolling countryside. First, our most famous battlefield, and second, the winter encampment of the Continental army — Gettysburg and Valley Forge — are still there to remind a sometimes-jaded citizenry of what some of our forebearers paid for dedication to a cause.

Most of Pennsylvania's border is a product of the surveyor's art, being perfectly regular on the north, south, and west. In the northwest a narrow chimney borders on Lake Erie. The state is otherwise saved from being a perfect rectangle by the Delaware River which cuts down from the Catskills of southern New York and through the Kittatinnies of Pennsylvania and New Jersey to form the grandly erratic eastern border. In a very general way, the Commonwealth of Pennsylvania may be divided into three regions as to topography. The southeast includes the plains and Piedmont country of the Delaware Valley as far west as the Blue Mountains. From the south-central border on up toward the northeast, the Alleghenies form a wide highland. The western third is high, rolling plateau, except for the plains of the Lake Erie shore.

The Pennsylvania scene is as varied as you could desire. It encompasses every conceivable kind of terrain except the extremes — such as the highest, lowest, wettest, driest, and so forth. Its natural resources are staggering. Some states far larger in area are poverty-stricken by comparison. Below ground are immense deposits of bituminous coal, high-quality coking coal west of the Alleghenies. Pennsylvania-grade oil comes from the west, too, a high-quality lubricating oil of unsurpassed excellence. In the east the coal mines around Scranton and Reading and Pottsville yield up the hard black rocks called anthracite. Clean-burning anthracite coal is found nowhere else in the world. But underground Pennsylvania is far from the whole story. The surface is no small potatoes, either, to use an agricultural image. The overlays of limestone soil in some parts of the state make farming an extremely worthwhile enterprise. Lancaster County, in the Pennsylvania Dutch country of the southeast, has outproduced any other area of equal size ever since the "Dutch" began farming it.

Half of Pennsylvania is covered by dense forests, both hardwoods and conifers. Its great range of plant life includes species that normally grow in other regions, as the South and the Mississippi Valley. The diversity of wildlife puts it in the front rank of states in this regard. Some of its larger animals, such as moose and elk, disappeared in the days when log-

9

ging and animal slaughter were unregulated. In this century the state has carried out extensive reforestation and reintroduced some vanished species. So the fishy, furry, and feathery kind are now deployed in strength throughout a vast and vigorous forest kingdom.

The extent of natural beauty in Pennsylvania is sometimes surprising to outsiders and visitors to the state. Even persons who were born there, including this writer, continue to be astonished by its visual enchantments. Such a situation seems to be helped along because lots of Pennsylvanians tend to cluster into a handful of bigger villages like Philadelphia, Pittsburgh, Erie, Harrisburg, Scranton, Allentown, and Altoona. That leaves the rest spread over a large area. So Pennsylvania has many small towns, some as old as the state itself, and which have remained small in all that time.

This, then, is the somewhat paradoxical Commonwealth of Pennsylvania. It has historically been a place of refuge for anyone seeking tolerance for a way of life and willing to allow others the same right. It is an old land and a new land. It is a jumble of factories and mines and crowded cities; and it is a quiet wilderness of lovely rivers, soft blue-green mountains, and pine-scented forests. It is truly a combination of many things, and in its contradictions and harmonies may, perhaps, be found the answer to the great spirit of the United States.

— P.M.L.

The Dynamic West

The western side of Pennsylvania has had, like the east, a crucial role in the state's development. Geographically, historically, and economically it has long been a keystone area of the Keystone State. In the 19th century Pennsylvania was the business leader of the nation. That preeminence came about, in part, because of the mineral and fossil fuel wealth that underlay its surface, particularly west of the Appalachians. Oil was discovered at Titusville, in the northwest, in 1859. Soon wells were drilled all over the upper western region, and the flow from them was enough for Pennsylvania to produce, up to the turn of the century, 60 percent of the nation's oil. Long before that the enormous bituminous coal fields of the "Pittsylvania country" had been discovered and were being worked. The coal vein underlying western Pennsylvania is so enormous that nearly all of the nation's production comes from this area along with West Virginia and Kentucky. The iron ores of the region, now pretty much depleted, helped launch Pittsburgh as the nation's "Steel City" in the last century. The area's steel mills now get their ores from out of state, some of them from the upper Michigan area. The oil fields long ago yielded supremacy to the giants of the Southwest, but Pennsylvania crude is still being pumped, its fine quality as a lubricating oil recognized in several well-known industry trade names.

All this should reinforce the point that western Pennsylvania represents wealth. Pittsburgh's strategic geographical position astride two rivers and at the head of a third, and its equally strategic position as a gateway to the interior of the country started it off with a flourish on its career as a center of industry. The competition of the railroad giants — the

Pennsylvania and the Baltimore & Ohio — to breach the Appalachians, and the activities of Andrew Carnegie, George Westinghouse, Andrew Mellon, and other financial and industrial wizards also helped establish the western region and Pittsburgh as a powerful center of commerce.

But the drive and the spirit of the people has been reflected in other ways besides the sober ones of business and industry. Reminders of some of the colorful events of the past are still very much in evidence. Take Brownsville, for example. It's an industrial town south of Pittsburgh on a hill by the Monongahela River. Last century it was busy forging iron. Before that, indeed, shortly after Brownsville became a town in 1785, a circle of communities in the area, with Brownsville taking the lead, launched the so-called Whiskey Rebellion in July, 1791. One of the chief products of the western country then was Monongahela rye. It was so plentiful that it was used as a medium of exchange. Farmers distilled it from corn, and the finished product was many times more valuable, by bulk, than the original grain. First the state, then the federal government, levied a tax on the whiskey. Not only did this cut into the profit from whiskey shipped across the mountains to the east, it taxed at a higher rate whiskey that was sold locally. Local leaders began to protest the excise as discriminatory: the rate was about a fourth of the selling price. So the Whiskey Rebellion was on. Besides Brownsville, Washington and Ginger Hill (now Slippery Rock) among other towns got into the act, refusing to pay the tax and roughing up the tax collectors. It was a very emotional issue, because whiskey was literally the life-blood of the people. The Whiskey Rebellion soon gave up, faced with opposition from Pittsburgh, which was in favor of the tax. The clincher was probably a massive show of force by the federal government. Some 13,000 troops were sent to Uniontown in 1794 to collect the tax and otherwise get things under control. Ginger Hill, by the way, was named for the practice of the town's tavern keeper of adding Jamaica ginger to the rye he dispensed.

Even with all the coal and oil in those hills, there is plenty of natural beauty to go around. In the north, smack in the middle of the oil and gas well region, is the 1,000-square-mile Allegheny National Forest. Most of this forest is, amazingly, prime woodland. Towns are present, but they are small and unobtrusive. Hundreds of miles of winding roads penetrate the forest, connecting the towns and providing access to recreation sites. Warren, one of Pennsylvania's big oil towns, is on its northern perimeter by the Allegheny River, which winds along the northern and western forest border. Kane is another community on the edge of the forest. On the eastern side nearer the mountains, it is one of the state's high-up towns, 2,013 feet in altitude. It makes a part of its living from Pittsburgh-area ski tourists who come to take advantage of its early snows.

Up in Pennsylvania's sawed-off northwestern panhandle is the Lake Erie plain, gently rolling farmland that ends on the lake shores. The city of Erie sits on these shores and keeps healthy from the heavy lake traffic into and out of its ports. Erie is a busy shipping and industrial town, but manages at the same time to maintain the serene look of a resort center. It makes a part of its living from Pittsburgh-area ski tourists who come to take advantage of its early snows.

Up in Pennsylvania's sawed-off northwestern panhandle is the Lake Erie plain, gently rolling farmland that ends on the lake shores. The city of Erie sits on these shores and keeps healthy from the heavy lake traffic into and out of its ports. Erie is a busy shipping and industrial town, but manages at the same time to maintain the serene look of a resort center. Its prime physical traits are spaciousness and generally low roof lines, even in its downtown district. It was planned along the lines of the national capital, and it preserves those lines even more fully than modern Washington does. It has great historic importance, too, in keeping with the Keystone State's crucial role in our early history. Presque Isle Peninsula, enclosing the city's landlocked harbor, was the launching pad for Oliver Hazard Perry's victorious encounter with British warships in Lake Erie during the War of 1812. One of the restored ships of Commodore Perry, the *Niagara*, is preserved on the Erie waterfront. And Presque Isle State Park, occupying the peninsula, further honors the naval hero with a victory monument. The peninsula's curving arm is furnished with beaches, woods, and ponds on its seven-mile length, making it a popular goal for recreationists during the summer.

Pittsburgh, they say, is the beginning and the end of all that happens in western Pennsylvania. Whether that is true to such an absolute degree is a question best left unanswered. The city at the confluence of the Three Rivers is, indeed, the centerpiece of a region that contains immense natural wealth and a large portion of rugged mountain and valley environment besides. Economically, geographically, and historically, Pittsburgh has been the fulcrum upon which everything else moves. Its vitality as a city has come from the great waves of ethnic groups flowing into it from other parts of the country and the world. The Germans, Lithuanians, Serbs, Hungarians, English, Scottish, Irish, Italians, and southerners, have come together there and created a city of great drive and enormous confidence in its abilities. Pittsburgh people are proud of their city — they even used to brag about the smoke and grime of its industrial district. But that brag is almost passé, because Pittsburgh a while back began to clean up. Its famed Golden Triangle, symbol of its industrial and financial might, today rises sharply etched in the newly-scrubbed air on the point of land formed by the converging Allegheny and Monongahela rivers. Pittsburgh has come a long way since the French and British were scuffling over whose fort it was back in the 1750s.

14

From the Piedmont To The Poconos

The Delaware Valley, with Philadelphia as its hub, spreads over the southeast corner of Pennsylvania, taking in four countries that fan out from the city like spokes of a wheel. It's part of the state where a web of highways ties together a thicket of residential and industrial centers that make up one of the world's biggest such concentrations of people. The Delaware river front, along most of this plain, has that man-made look that big port complexes have in our day and age. Shipyards, steel mills, factories, oil refineries, and giant piers elbow each other for riverbank space. Close to four million people have crowded together in this corner, so it would seem unlikely that much open space would remain. Yet it does, in the big city itself, in the stylish and beautiful suburbs on the north and west, and in the far edges of the four surrounding counties, where the rolling Piedmont country begins.

The carefully preserved open spaces within this urban complex may, sometimes, owe their natural beauty to what happened there before we were yet a nation. Valley Forge is one of these places, both beautiful and sacred. Now a state park, the rolling valley has been frozen in time much as it was during that heroic winter encampment of Washington's patriot army in December of 1777. Now, as then, the snow sometimes comes in deep drifts during the winter, piling against today's replicas of the soldiers' crude log huts, as it did against the originals during that winter of hardship. Now the campground is close by the bulging limits of Philadelphia, but still aloof from that town where the British were so comfortably garrisoned after having defeated the Continentals at Brandywine and Germantown. When it is not winter at Valley Forge, the outlook is green and glorious. The hills around it are crowded with oaks and maples; around its northern perimeter flows the big, fast-moving Schuylkill (pronounced Skook'l) River, now paralleled by the big, fast-moving Schuylkill Expressway into Philadelphia.

Other reminders of the Revolution crowd into this corner of Pennsylvania. Southwest of Philadelphia some 30 miles is Brandywine Creek. Just before the stream enters the state of Delaware, on its way to the river of that name, is the town of Chadds Ford, on the east bank. Here is where the Battle of Brandywine took place on September 11, 1777, when Washington and his outnumbered army tried unsuccessfully to prevent the British from taking Philadelphia. The Brandywine battlefield today is more concerned with conservation than maneuvers. Its soft, rolling hills and the big, old maple and sycamore trees, lining the now-diminished creek, have been organized into the Brandywine Conservation Area, a managed mixture of contour farms and wildlife ponds. This is where the Brandywine school of artists holds forth. The Brandywine River Museum, a restored gristmill in Chadds Ford, is the setting for paintings of this kind by the Wyeths and Howard Pyle.

Eleuthere Irenée du Pont de Nemours founded the Du Pont dynasty with his gunpowder mills along the Brandywine. His descendants have enriched the state of Pennsylvania with one of the world's most extensive botanical collections. Longwood Gardens, near Chadds Ford in this lovely old-world countryside, combine outdoor gardens, arboretums, fountains, and greenhouses with thousands of different kinds of exotic plants. It's all open to the public at no charge.

To the north, on the other side of Philadelphia, is another hallowed site, like Valley Forge, a state park. Washington Crossing Park commemorates the time and the location of the indomitable general's crossing of the Delaware with his incredible, never-say-die little army to capture Trenton, New Jersey, from the Hessians. Every school child knows the story of that surprise maneuver, carried out during snowy December — Christmas night, 1776. On the river bank where Washington actually em-

Brady's Lake, Pocono Mountains

Bridalveil Falls, Bushkill Falls

Sachs Mill Bridge near Gettysburg

Near New Lexington

Independence Hall, Philadelphia

Hyner's Vista, 2,000 feet above the Susquehanna River

Hopewell Village

Spring Mount, Pennsylvania

Minister Creek, Western Pennsylvania

Philadelphia

Autumn near Bedford

Allegheny Reservoir, Allegheny National Forest

Autumn comes to the Pocono Mountains

Susquehanna River near Azilum

Bedford County Covered Bridge #18

State Capitol Building, Harrisburg

Near Troy, Pennsylvania

Soldiers' National Monument, Gettysburg

Allegheny River from Tidioute Overlook

Gettysburg Area Farm

Lower Gorge Falls at Bushkill Falls

Lake Erie, near Erie

Gettysburg Area farm

Near Lancaster

Near Montoursville

Valley Forge Memorial Park

Longwood Gardens

McConnell's Mill State Park

Gettysburg National Military Park

Bucks County

Creek near Ursina

George Washington's Headquarters at Valley Forge

Farm Country near Williamport

Near Wilmot

Pittsburgh

Near Uniontown

Cucumber Falls, Ohiopyle State Park

Pennsylvania Dutch Country near Lancaster

Ben Franklin Bridge, Philadelphia

Hans Herr House (1719) Lancaster County

McConnell's Mill State Park

Knox Covered Bridge near Valley Forge

Allegheny River

Ohiopyle Falls, Youghiogheny River

Near Towanda

Stover-Myers Mill, Bucks County

The "Devil's Backbone," near Erie

Lake Arthur Sunset

barked, now stands a Memorial Building containing the emotion-stirring painting by Emanuel Leutze of that epochal event. Buildings preserved and restored from that long-ago time occupy the area. One of these is the big farmhouse, dating from 1702, where Washington planned his daring raid. Another is the Old (Grist) Mill that ground wheat for the Continental Army, the mill's ponderous water wheel still turned by the waters of a creek. More than a million visitors are drawn to this place every year, some of them on Christmas Day, when it all happens again, with actors in Colonial uniforms making the trip in a boat like Washington's.

The countryside from Philadelphia north toward Easton is a patchwork of mellow vistas that yield to no other part of the country for pure, shameless beauty. Bucks County, lying along the river on the north edge of the city, accomplishes all this by natural charm overlaid with a lot of history. Washington Crossing is one of its special places, as we have just seen. Another is New Hope, a few miles up the Delaware. The little writers' and artists' colony in wooded hills dates from Revolutionary times and has a settled-in look that is reminiscent of European towns. Many of its old buildings have been converted to use as shops and restaurants. The historic Delaware Canal glides through the town, reaching into upper Bucks County. The 50-mile-long canal was opened in 1830 as a link in the water route from Lake Erie to the ports of Philadelphia and New York. Now it carries only visitors and sightseers along its placid green banks in barges pulled by mules plodding along the well-trod towpath. Above New Hope, Bucks County is a photogenic world of little valleys that drop steeply to dark and cool floors, where clear streams chatter briskly or softly murmur on their way to the Delaware River. Further inland the Bucks countryside is dotted with villages where stone houses and whitewashed barns sit by rushing creeks in settings that evoke the spirit of past time.

Even the very heart of Philadelphia itself has its open space. The most noteworthy example of this is Fairmount Park, a huge reserve where William Penn's idea of a "Greene countrie towne" seems to be fulfilled. The park stretches for several miles over the hills along both sides of the Schuylkill River in west-central Philadelphia and for several more miles along Wissahickon Creek to the north. The park is maintained in as natural a state as possible. Its trees and dells, creeks and rocky outcroppings flank the river and creek with soul-restoring beauty in the midst of the city's tight concentrations of residential neighborhoods. Man-made beauty finds a sanctuary in the park, too. A great number of statues and outdoor sculptures are found along the park drives. The Fairmount Park mansions, administered and maintained by the Philadelphia Museum of Art, date from the Colonial and Revolutionary periods. These elegant homes were once owned and lived in by important figures of the nation's early days, such as Robert Morris and Benedict Arnold.

Most Americans know that Philadelphia's core area is filled with some of the nation's most sacred relics and hallowed buildings. The "old city" near the Delaware River is known as the Birthplace of the Nation, and rightly so. Here Independence National Historical Park provides a well-groomed setting for some of our most famous old buildings, including, of course, Independence Hall. The center city in the years following World War II has been undergoing a massive face-lifting. The result is a handsome and revitalized core where open space is abundant and the mellow look of former times has returned. Just one street remains with the cramped scale of its beginnings in the 1700s. This is Elfreth's Alley, just off Independence Park near the river. The cobblestone street, looking like a setting for a Dickens novel, is only six feet wide, its tiny houses huddled against each other as if for support. In June Philadelphia observes Elfreth's Alley Day, when the old street holds open house, to music from a fife and drum corps. It's another way Philadelphia remembers and honors its past, while making bold moves in the present toward creating a better "Greene countrie towne."

Farther west, in southeastern Pennsylvania, is the stronghold of the world-famous Pennsylvania Dutch. The "Dutch" are really German in origin, descendants of sectarian refugees from the Rhineland who came to Penn's liberal lands in the early and middle 18th century in order to practice their beliefs in peace. The so-called Pennsylvania Dutch have established themselves as the world's best farmers in some of the world's best farming country. Regardless of their strict or not-so-strict beliefs and practices, they have been an extremely valuable and productive element in the life of the state and the nation. Three Pennsylvania counties are best known as "Dutch" country: Berks, Lebanon, and Lancaster. Here the Germanic influence and traditions are best observed in the small villages, such as Millersville and Manheim, Ephrata, Hamburg, Kutztown, and Emmaus, even though the bigger "Dutch" towns like Lancaster, Lebanon, Reading, and Allentown have made more of a tourist attraction out of the Dutch culture.

Not only the eye but the nose can appreciate the rich textures of the Dutch country. Undulating fields and aromatic barnyards are a sensory treat. Everything has a prosperous, well-tended appearance, from the spacious, hipped-roof farm buildings to the neat fields and sleek livestock. The healthy looking farm families are their own advertisement for their prosperity. Sometimes the red barns have hex signs on them in a variety of colorful red, blue, and white geometrical designs. The hex circles are more for decoration these days than anything else, but a little crop insurance doesn't hurt.

The most readily identifiable sect of all has a large representation in the Lancaster-Reading area. The strict observance of practices deriving from the sect's beginnings still is the rule in the daily lives of the Amish. The city of Lancaster has some farmers' markets where the "Plain People," as they are called, come in their somber clothing to sell their produce, the women in their bonnets, the men with their beards and broad-brimmed hats. Even the children are dressed the same way, looking like pint-sized versions of the grownups. The farm crops will probably have arrived at the stalls by horse and buggy, for the Amish still refuse to own automobiles. Even on their farms, the usages of the 20th century are disdained. The very strictest families ban photographs, mirrors, and indoor plumbing as "vanities" not in accord with their religious beliefs.

On the eastern limits of the Poconos flows the Delaware, dividing Pennsylvania from New Jersey and cutting through the neighboring Kittatinny Mountains that range through both states. Where the notch is made, the Delaware has fashioned a majestic tableau that is one of the

While becoming settled by German refugees, this corner of Pennsylvania was also involved in the Revolution, and some artifacts of that time are still around. One of these is Hopewell Furnace, in French Creek State Park near Reading. The forge and Revolutionary-era Hopewell Village have been restored as a National Historic Site. It was one of the suppliers of cannonballs to the Continental Army. Name-dropping is a legitimate activity in this hilly country; Daniel Boone was born here, and his family homestead is preserved not far from French Creek Park. Boone's father, a Quaker, is believed to have built part of the brownstone house in the 1730s. Before the Hopewell people thought of cannonballs, and possibly before the elder Mr. Boone thought of Daniel, somebody unknown in the Conestoga Valley south of Lancaster invented a big, hefty wagon to take care of the growing freight needs of the Philadelphia-Lancaster link. The famed Conestoga became the country's transportation of choice for more than a century, reincarnated as the prairie schooner later on when migration pushed out into the Far West.

Northeast Pennsylvania is a mountain-and-lake kingdom with a distinctly different "feel" from the high country in the central part of the state. These are the Poconos, lower than some of the more remote ridges around the state, and probably a tamer wilderness (but the mountain lions occasionally seen there might argue the point). Lakes are everywhere in these gentle elevations, adding a fresh, cool ingredient to the pine-scented Pocono air even on the hottest days. Lately, the winter bird and wildlife of the Poconos have had to share their living quarters with people who have discovered that the slopes around here are just right for ski runs. These handy mountains have become a favorite recreational retreat for people from eastern Pennsylvania, northern New Jersey, and southern New York.

Pennsylvania's scenic masterpieces. The beautiful gorge is called the Delaware Water Gap, slicing between two fault blocks 1,200 feet high. The Appalachian Trail goes by here, high on the mountain shoulders. A few miles away from the Gap is another of the state's old historic towns. Stroudsberg started as a stockade in 1776, built by Colonel Jacob Stroud, a veteran of the French and Indian War. Stroudsberg became a Moravian town, while serving as a haven for Revolutionary casualties. Its location amidst the Pocono-Kittatinny mountains and valleys makes it especially attractive to visitors, and adds dollars to the local treasury. In autumn the mountain slopes around it are ablaze with the russet tones of turning foliage.

Big Pocono State Park, a few miles to the west, is a good place to become acquainted with the fabulous old geology revealed on the rock walls of about every cut for a road made in these mountains. Big Pocono is 2,131 feet tall, the worn-down nub of something that is supposed to have been about 40,000-feet tall at some legendary time before the Rockies were ever thought of. There are coral rock and marine fossils in these hills, proving that seas washed over the land in some impossibly ancient era. Not-so-ancient glaciers crushed down from the north more than once, probably. The lakes that show up everywhere are creatures of the glaciers, which carved out lake beds as they retreated from a warming climate. Bruce Lake is one of these, a 48-acre jewel within a large natural area next to Promised Land State Park in the Poconos. The lake is unreachable by roads, and accessible only by trail. One of the most enjoyable experiences, available from many high points along the Pocono and Kittatinny ridges, are the long views of myriad ranges and rolling hills to the far horizon. Three states come within the eye's compass on the highest points, as also, on some occasions, ever-changing perspectives of the nearby Delaware Water Gap itself.

The Pocono playground is all the more remarkable for its nearness to the famed anthracite coal fields of the state. The Poconos — mountains and plateau — practically skirt the big coal towns of Scranton and Wilkes-

Barre and smaller ones like Carbondale and Honesdale. Yet their psychological distance from those nearby industrial areas on the west is immense, their gentle wilderness quite a miraculous instance of beauty and utility existing compatibly in close proximity.

The Delaware River flows big and broad and business-like past the industrial docksides of lower Pennsylvania and New Jersey, but the upper river is another creature. As it begins to carve out that wriggly eastern border of the state, it is very much a sparkling mountain stream, casting glittery lights off its blue waters. Sometimes it's a green river, reflecting the dense woods and shrubs of the bankside. Cutting through the long, green-forested mountain ridges, the Delaware pours over rocks and ledges and shows off its shallow bed through limpid waters. The plentiful fish attract fishing birds: herons, kingfishers, mergansers. Along this narrow upper river, the natural scene is in charge, with very few evidences of human activity. Riverbank towns of this corner county (Wayne) are tiny and infrequent. The stretch of river they sit on has been involved in the affairs of a nation for a long time, in peace and war. The French and Indian wars seesawed through these mountains and forests and along this river. Some of these Wayne County communities were close to the action, and some of their citizens were involved on either one or the other side of the skirmishes.

The estate of Gifford Pinchot, Pennsylvania governor in the 20s, reminds Pennsylvanians of Pinchot's wide-ranging conservation interests, both as governor and as Director of Forestry in the Theodore Roosevelt and Taft administrations. The estate is in Milford, a lower Wayne County town that hangs over the Delaware on a bluff. Now the Institute for Conservation Studies, it focuses interest on nature. One of Pennsylvania's most photogenic cataracts, Saw Kill Falls, is here. It plunges over a 60-foot-wide rock wall in a fern-bedecked forest, falling in 75 feet of spray down to a shadowy green chasm. Nature is a bit managed on this 101-acre estate but there's nothing wrong with that, when it's done with such great understanding and feeling for man's best kind of relationship with his natural surroundings.

70

Of Mountains
And a River

From north border to south border, central Pennsylvania is an Oz-like complication of mountainous ridges, rolling plateau, quicksilver streams, and one grand river that rolls through its heart like an artery that keeps things in good working order. The Susquehanna is, indeed, the life-blood of the rugged interior. Not navigable except by shallow-draft vessels, it is nevertheless a big water-carrier, a mile wide in its lower reaches around Harrisburg. Its beautiful Indian name is, supposedly, a comment on how it looks after a hard rain. It means "muddy river." The Susquehanna is fed by countless mountain creeks or "runs" pouring down the countless ridges the river twists around. One major tributary, the Juniata, comes in from the west, north of Harrisburg.

Two arms of the Susquehanna, the West Branch and the North Branch, sweep through west-central and northern Pennsylvania. They combine at Northumberland and Sunbury to form the main stem that winds through Pennsylvania, eastern Maryland for a short stint, then out into Chesapeake Bay. Ever since people began to live in what is now Pennsylvania, the river and its wide, fertile valley have been a controlling factor in their lives. Some of the earliest settlers along the Susquehanna were the Susquehannocks, part of the so-called Iroquois confederated nations who took a stance of independence from, and indeed hatred of, Iroquois rule. They settled on the lower river, spreading out as far south as the Chesapeake Bay area. Until the latter part of the 17th century, they had defeated all Iroquois efforts to subdue them. But they gradually succumbed to Iroquois raids and the pressure of white settlers along the West

Branch, where they had retreated in the 1760s. Their numbers diminished until they were extinguished as a separate Indian tribe.

Early fur trappers were the first Europeans in the Susquehanna Valley. After William Penn received his charter for Pennsylvania in 1681, settlers began arriving in the new colony in large numbers. By the mid-eighteenth century, they had spread to the lower Susquehanna and up along the main river to Shamokin (now Sunbury). As the century entered its second half, the North Branch of the upper river began to acquire both Pennsylvania and Connecticut settlers. The Wyoming Valley along the river was an area of conflict between the two groups. The Yankee invaders began farming the fertile soil but were forced by Pennsylvania troops on five separate occasions to retire to their rocky home colony. Some of the encounters were marked by great bloodshed. They lasted through the Revolution and into the 1780s. The famous Wyoming Massacre occurred during the Revolutionary period, when most of the Yankee settlements in the valley were destroyed by a New York alliance of British and Indians, and their inhabitants killed or captured.

The Wyoming Valley has been known both as the Great Warrior Path and Sullivan's Trail, the latter name attaching to it because of a successful punitive expedition carried out by General John Sullivan, under Washington's command, against the British and Iroquois involved in the Wyoming Massacre. Today, the North Branch, curving in a giant arc as it comes south from New York past Scranton and Wilkes-Barre, has been designated a federal "scenic river." It is one of today's miracle rivers, one of the longest stretches of running water left unpolluted in the East.

Harrisburg, on the east bank of the Susquehanna's main stem at the edge of the mountain country, was "launched," one might say, as a ferry stop and trading post much earlier in the 18th century. The town, itself, was not established until 1785, by the son of the original founder of the post, and named after him. Harrisburg's strategic position and its magnificent Susquehanna location brought it into contention for selection in 1789 as the new nation's capital city. The national congress in that year

72

finally chose Washington on the Potomac. Harrisburg became Pennsylvania's capital in 1812.

When Harris's Ferry was laid out as a town, the state legislature made it the county seat of Dauphin County, the latter name reflecting the influence of French immigration during the French Revolution. The legislature then named the town Louisbourg, after Louis XVI. But John Harris, Jr., rose up in righteous wrath and refused to sell any more of his land for a town "except in Harrisburg." His ultimatum changed the legislative mind. The Harris family name was restored to the town and has remained. What has also remained is Harrisburg's great good looks, a combination of natural gifts and careful planning. The city's broad river drive lined with big old trees and magnificent homes gives it a regal dignity. The final touch is the ornate Italian Renaissance capitol building, its dome rising majestically from the high perspective of hills back of the river. Harrisburg was and is a quiet place. It partakes of the Pennsylvania Dutch home-loving state of mind. The fair city's peace has only once been in some danger of being interrupted and her noble vistas threatened. That was during the Civil War when Robert E. Lee's Confederate armies reached the outskirts, only to turn south to Gettysburg, where the climactic battle of the war was fought.

Gettysburg is across the river, in the history-laden countryside of south-central Pennsylvania. The "Dutch" are well represented here, too, in the York and Hanover precincts. York, founded in 1741, was the first settlement west of the Susquehanna. It was the home of the Continental Congress during the British occupation of Philadelphia after the Brandywine campaign. A century later Gettysburg became the scene of another war in these southern Pennsylvania foothills. The area's serene beauty today makes all the more poignant its role in one of the Civil War's most terrible battles. More than four-million visitors each year come to Gettysburg's woods-studded vale and wander over the battlefield and the hallowed ground of the National Military Park. At a fancy new Visitor Center, they hear about that incredible struggle on July 2, 3, and 4, 1863, when the fortunes of the Union and the Confederacy hung in the balance. For 50-thousand men, Gettysburg was the last battle. Some 2,300 monuments studding the battlefield's 16,000 rolling acres contribute powerfully toward a feeling for what happened there not so long ago. In the National Cemetery of the battlefield park, the Soldier's National Monument marks the site of some brief remarks by Abraham Lincoln at the dedication ceremonies. Of all the marvelously wrought monuments to those who fought there, the most complete and perfect is that little two-minute speech — the President's Gettysburg Address.

South-central Pennsylvania is in the thick of the mountains' march through the state. The ridges of the Tuscarora and Blue mountains stretch for many miles like giant waves following one upon the other. In long views across blue-green valleys, the land merges with a hazy-purple horizon. Cowans Gap State Park, high in the Tuscaroras, is a typical beauty spot in these rugged and heavily forested mountains, profuse with wildflowers at some times of the year. These little, sheltered mountain valleys sometimes have a story to tell that goes hand-in-hand with the scenery. More than 200 years ago, Cowans Gap was homesteaded by Samuel Cowan, a young British officer, and his bride from Boston. She remained in this bird- and flower-filled, creek-watered spot until long after his death, and was discovered at the age of 102 by a surveying party.

The West Branch is the less settled arm of the Susquehanna. It cuts into the heart of the Allegheny Mountains from a beginning far into the western side of the Pennsylvania rectangle. Unlike the North Branch, much of its course is through deep wilderness. Its valley is very much little-town territory, with communities 200 and more years old. This is central Pennsylvania, another distinct part of the state. Its big towns are Williamsport, an historic old community and former lumber center on the West Branch; Sunbury, where the West and North branches meet; State College, in Centre County; and Lewistown, on the Juniata River, a gorgeous stream that cuts through some of the complicated ridges between here and Mifflintown to form a four-mile-long wooded gorge called the Lewistown Narrows. All of these towns, big as they are today, are absorbed into their river or mountain settings with no noticeable loss to the lush charms of the natural background.

The "Dutch" are found here, too. Their presence is felt in the look of the small towns, in the look of the people, in the rich agricultural lands outside of the towns. For, although this mountainous region is less fertile than the rich limestone hills around Lancaster and Lebanon, there is still a lot of farming that gets done. In this part of Pennsylvania, where the broken terrain seems almost independent of the ruling stream that is the upper West Branch, the towns are minor interruptions in the midst of rolling fields of corn and wheat. The forests seem to be everywhere else, wherever a slope begins to rise into the wall of surrounding ridges. Where the towns are, they line up along the highway, which somehow is transformed when it enters the community. The houses, some clapboard, some brick or stone, snuggle up close to the street, wide porches running along the front and sometimes around the sides. Mellow-looking red brick churches and unobtrusive shops are found in the core areas. The sidewalks are narrow and the main street through town curves and dips to follow the rolling landscape. They are friendly places. If you take a walk through them, everybody, the porch sitters and pedestrians, will say hello as you pass. Strangers may get a little more attention than townspeople, and a warm welcome is practically guaranteed.

Central Pennsylvania offers great adventure to the visitor of its mountains and valleys. That initial excitement is experienced when the first range of mountains shows up across the river from Harrisburg.

Going up the east bank north of the city, the highway passes the stone-arch Rockville Bridge, carrying the Pennsylvania Railroad tracks across the Susquehanna. The bridge, stepping over the mile-wide river on ponderous legs, is the longest of its kind in the world. Twelve miles north of Harrisburg, at Clark's Ferry, it's possible to cross the river (on a bridge, not a ferry) and head up the west bank at Amity Hall, once important as the intersection point of Pennsylvania's east-west and north-south canal systems. Now Amity Hall is a popular stop for highway travelers. One attention getter north of Amity Hall is Girty's Face, a natural cliff formation along the road, looking like the long-nosed face of a man. The cliff has been traditionally known as Girty's Face, named after Simon Girty, a renegade Revolutionary soldier who joined up with the Indians and is supposed to have hidden in a nearby mountain cave.

Some 15 miles south of Selinsgrove, the river route may be abandoned for a state route that cuts cross-country to US Highway 45, just west of Mifflinsburg. It's worth a short backtrack just for a look at the prosperous "Dutch" farming and mill town. From the tiny village of Hartleton, the road lifts a long grade into Bald Eagle State Forest, high on Paddy Mountain. This route through dense pine forests is called the Seven-Mile Narrows, and leads through some of Pennsylvania's wildest and most spectacular forest and mountain country. You can almost become intoxicated by the incredible pine woods fragrance, almost as thick as syrup as it hangs in the air.

The eyes get a workout, too, gazing at the green and dark forests stretching endlessly back from the road. The Narrows is rather like a roller coaster, a curving, up-and-down defile through the mountain. This wilderness shelters an abundance of wildlife, from deer to raccoon, bear, fox, beaver, and wildcat. (Pennsylvania harbors more wild animals than any other north-eastern state, and a great many of them roam these high ridges and deep valleys of the West Branch's domain.) Once through the Narrows, it's a drop into Penn's Valley for the last few miles to Millheim. At the bottom of the mountain is the hamlet of Woodward, so tiny that you can hold your breath when entering and not breathe again until you have passed through. Woodward is the gateway to Woodward Cave, one of the state's biggest dry caverns.

Millheim and Aaronsburg, two Penn Valley towns almost next door to each other on US Highway 45, are very small, typical in that respect at least of interior Pennsylvania's many Germanic settlements. Most villages are widely spaced through the valleys. Aaronsburg is the older of the two, laid out before 1775 by Aaron Levy of Sunbury. Aaronsburg, in its own deep little vale, once had ideas of becoming the state capital city. Wide setbacks and spacious lawns line the main street as it dips through town.

Millheim, just over the next hill, is also cupped in a little hollow. On a bike or a good pair of roller skates, you can start at the eastern end and roll right into the center of town. I know. I used to do it, out on the road, in a day when there weren't so many cars.

Farther west is State College, now known by University Park. It is a college town, as you may have guessed. Nittany Mountain is somewhere in the vicinity, thus the name Nittany Lions for Pennsylvania State University's nationally fearsome football heroes who sharpen their claws on this sylvan campus preparatory to mauling the opposition in the annual autumn frolics. Bellefonte, nearby to the northeast, snuggles up against long Bald Eagle Mountain. The town's name means "beautiful fountain" in French. Supposedly the French statesman Talleyrand is responsible for it, having made such a pronouncement when he saw the town's Big Spring while on a visit here during his exile from France in 1794-5. The Big Spring is still a *belle fonte*, pouring forth 11-million gallons daily of pure, cold mountain water. Limestone deposits in the area make up Bellefonte's industrial base, and the town is also a center for hunters, fishermen, and farmers. Streets leading from the main thoroughfare literally climb up the side of the mountain, where houses hang on sometimes improbable-looking perches.

Centre County and the counties around it are filled with a wide assortment of mountain and creek wildernesses, some of them within the confines of state parks and recreation areas. Pennsylvanians like to remember the famous people, like Talleyrand, who visited or lived in the state for a time, and one of the softly beautiful places in this mountain country is named for an illustrious man of letters. Poe Valley, just over the mountain south of Penn's Valley, honors Edgar Allen Poe, the builder of gothic poems and stories. Poe lived in Philadelphia for a while, and during that time visited with a relative who had settled in the valley area. Poe Valley is out in the woods all by itself, watered by Penn's Creek and Little Poe Creek. It is here that the poet is believed to have written *The Raven*. The valley is a lovely, lonely glade where two state recreation areas, Poe Valley State Park and Poe Paddy Park, now offer a broad range of nature experiences. From a high ridge here, Penn's View, famous all over the state for its stunning purple-mountain vistas, looks north to Bald Eagle Mountain and beyond. Mixed pine and hardwood forests swarm over the interwoven ridges far into the distance. The patented beauty of the scene varies with the seasonal color changes, but in one way it is always the same: awesome.

Penn's View doesn't quite reach up to north-central Pennsylvania, and more's the pity. Here is the state's high plateau country, where autumn colors, when autumn comes, are arranged in a different perspective. Due north from Poe country some 60 miles in a straight line is Pennsylvania's "Grand Canyon," cut by 100-mile-long Pine Creek that eventually reaches down to the West Branch of the Susquehanna. At Leonard Harrison and Colton Point state parks, flanking the gorge a few miles southwest of Wellsboro, the visitor may perch on the edge and direct his gaze downward a thousand feet, watching Pine Creek still at work. The steep, forested walls of the chasm are resplendent on a crisp fall day, in gold and scarlet. The red-tailed hawk is king here; he soars over a magnificent 50-mile-long gorge, his echoing cry mingling with the splash of the rushing creek. This was once one of the East's most heavily logged mountain chasms, white pine stripped from the slopes as if there were no tomorrow, and floated down Pine Creek. The area's fall colors are in part a legacy of the New Englanders who settled in north-central Pennsylvania for a while in the late 18th century, determined to annex the region to Connecticut. They brought their elms and sugar maples and planted them in and around towns. Wellsboro, the gateway to the canyon, has many of these aged trees. The Yankees also raised houses in the New England architectural style, and Wellsboro's architecture still reflects this influence with its Greek Revival columned porticos. The skirmishes between the New Englanders and the Pennsylvanians over this part of the state gave way after a while to the more critical business of starting a new nation. But this early incursion by the Connecticut Yankees has left a rich vein of New England that makes this spectacular forest and canyon country even more interesting than nature did all by herself.